Poems

# The Borders

*Selected by* Amy Wack

Seren is the book imprint of
Poetry Wales Press Ltd.
57 Nolton Street, Bridgend, Wales, CF31 3AE

www.serenbooks.com
facebook.com/SerenBooks
twitter@SerenBooks

ISBN: 978-1-78172-487-3

A CIP record for this title is available from the British Library.

The publisher acknowledges the financial assistance of the Welsh Books Council.

Cover photograph: © Barry Needle / Hay on Wye

Printed in the Czech Republic by Akcent Media Ltd.

# Contents

# *Acknowledgements*

We gratefully acknowledge the permission of the publishers of the titles from which these poems are taken:

**Christopher Meredith**: 'Borderland' from *Air Histories*, (Seren, 2013); **Elizabeth Parker**: 'Home to the Garden Centre: in the Forest of Dean' from *In Her Shambles*, (Seren, 2018); **Emma van Woerkom**: 'Brechfa Pool' and 'Water Break-its-Neck' – new poems; **Owen Sheers**: 'Skirrid Fawr' from *Skirrid Hill*, (Seren, 2000); **Rhiannon Hooson**: 'Luminosity' from *The Other City,* (Seren, 2017); **Nicholas Whitehead**: 'Hiders' new poem; **Paul Deaton**: 'Red Brick Farm' from *A Watchful Astronomy*, (Seren, 2017); **Ric Hool**: 'Thigh-deep in Snow & Thinking: Lee Harwood', first published 2012 in *Tears In The Fence 54* and *A way of Falling Upwards*, (Cinnamon Press, 2014); **Paul Groves**: 'At Partrishow in the Black Mountains' from *Wowsers*, (Seren, 2002); **Ruth Bidgood**: 'Edward Bache Advises His Sister' from *Selected Poems*, (Seren, 2004); **Maggie Harris**: 'Slave Bangle, Wales' from *Sixty Years of Loving*, (Guyana Prize, 2014, Cane Arrow Press); **John Barnie**: 'Where I'm From' new poem; **Barney Norris**: 'Crickadarn' new poem; **Simon Mundy**: 'Winter Treachery at Gwaithla' from *More for Helen of Troy*, (Seren, 2012); **John Powell Ward**: 'The Wye Below Bredwardine' from *Selected and New Poems*, (Seren, 2004); **Tracey Rhys**: 'En Route to Hay' new poem; **Ben Ray**: 'Talybont to Llangattock' new poem; **Gareth Writer-Davies**: 'Mushrooms' Winner of the Prole Laureate 2017 Competition; **Catherine Fisher**: 'Severn Bore' from *Immrama*, (Seren, 1988); **Philip Gross**: 'Severn Song' from *The Water Table*, (Bloodaxe, 2009); **Claire Williamson**: 'Llancaut/Llan Cewydd' new poem; **Paul Henry**: 'Boy Running' from *Boy Running*, (Seren, 2016); **Nicholas Murray**: 'Yggdrasil' from *Planet,* no 224, 2016 and reprinted in *The Museum of Truth* (Melos, 2018); **Richard Gwyn**: 'Border Country' first published in an earlier version: 'Waking' in *Walking on Bones* (Parthian, 2000); **Fiona Sampson**: 'Montgomery Orchard' new poem; **Charles Wilkinson**: 'Englynion with Gnomes and Butterflies' first appeared in *Envoi*; **Jonathan Edwards**: 'Anatomy' from *My Family and Other Superheroes*, (Seren, 2014).

*Christopher Meredith*

# BORDERLAND

*Ffin is Welsh for border. It occurs inside* diffiniad *which means definition, and in Capel y Ffin, a place in the Black Mountains.*

You'll find a *ffin* inside each definition.
We see what is when we see what it's not:
edges are where meanings happen.

On the black whaleback of this mountain
earth curves away so sky can start
to show a *ffin's* a kind of definition

where skylarks climb across earth's tun
to air and pulsing muscle turns to an art-
ful song the edge that lets a meaning happen.

Live rock can yield to mortared stone,
a city to a castle, then a shepherd's hut,
where *ffin's* contained inside a definition,

where the lithic turns into the human.
Here's where things fall together, not apart
at edges that let meanings happen.

And self here blurs into annihilation.
Larkfall, earthfall, skyfall, manfall each create
the *ffin* that is the place of definition
the edges where we see our meanings happen.

*Elizabeth Parker*

# HOME TO THE GARDEN CENTRE: THE FOREST OF DEAN

We return when the garden flares
red, pink, orange rhododendrons and camellias,
hydrangeas freeing their blue moths

to nestcones spit-stitched to the eaves,
the gargoyle with moss on his hands,
a nostril plugged with lichen.

We return to paths ribbed with sleepers,
bogey wheels spiked with cogs
rusting on stream banks

to locked coalmines,
unworked, cream-faced quarries,
a forest still oozing iron,
bedrocks greased with ore.

We return to boss-eyed boar rutting on the verge,
piglets with humbug stripes

to hunting, saltlicks, culls,
white flickers
in the tails of fallow deer.

We return to the stuccoed house,
two miners' cottages knocked through

the stutter of her Singer
as she hems liberty prints for curtains, cushion covers,
foot dipping, rising on the treadle.

We return to her ceramic bowl
beside the Belfast sink

shaped like a bellflower,
black with tadpoles every spring

their mouths opening holes in the surface,
their tiny sucks on our fingertips.

*Emma van Woerkom*

# BRECHFA POOL

Brechfa Pool, what do you know?
Each summer you shrink into yourself – gilding a year's tittle-tattle in hill-silver.
The feigned whisperings of lapwings, the crimson thirsts of crooked thorns
or the vanities of sheep. Each sipped through the tightening lips of
barely opened mouths. Yet here you loll. Pulled back from
the edges. Rolled-over, tucked-under, gathered-up
in tales and your poker-face which never
fails – a blown pupil taking us all
in. Warping our visions in
partitions of sky, till we
are wild-eyed for
your perfect,
perfect
light.

*Owen Sheers*

# SKIRRID FAWR

Just like the farmers who once came to scoop
handfuls of soil from her holy scar,

so I am still drawn to her back for the answers
to every question I have never known.

To the sentence of her slopes,
the blunt wind glancing from her withers,

to the split view she reveals
with every step along her broken spine.

This edge of her cleft palate,
part hill, part field,

rising from a low mist, a lonely hulk
adrift through Wales.

Her east-west flanks, one dark, one sunlit,
her vernacular of borders.

Her weight, the unspoken words
of an unlearned tongue.

# Rhiannon Hooson
# LUMINOSITY

*A visit to Blackwardine led me to note on the map a straight line starting from Croft Ambury*
*...and through the high ground at Stretton Grandison, where I surmise a Roman station. I followed*
*up the clue of sighting from hilltop, unhampered by other theories, found it yielding astounding results*
*in all districts, the straight lines to my amazement passing over and over again through the same class*
*of objects.* (from *Early British Trackways*, Alfred Watkins 1922)

Light always travels in a straight line
until you coax it elsewhere, and then
it flows like water, dripping from sills
and organising shadows into watersheds.

Other days it's frozen into rods, straight
as string for measuring. Nothing could stop it
then, only tinge it temporarily until the flood
of it crashed coloured through a window.

And there was a day, late June, walking
the marches when light resolved itself for you,
beamed across the landscape with sudden ferocity
so that everything became meaningful: barrows

stood proud of their sunken roots, the tall stones
announced themselves across the hills and you
were struck straight through with the simple, complex
web of it. Only later did you think of Hermes,

that subtle god of between-places, and of men
lighting beacons on the mountain-tops each spring
fires burning in a chain, horizon to horizon,
thrusting up light to the stars like an echo.

And only then walked the old straight track back
to Blackwardine, seeing in each stride another mile
breached by nameless men, a flare of sight, as if
you were seeing all the land in the world at once.

## Nicholas Whitehead

# HIDERS

No-one knows he's here. In Jell's café
for eccentrics in Llandrindod Wells,
the man with the chocolate-chip voice is
Alexis Korner. Godfather to the Rolling Stones.

No-one knows she's here. Talking anti-nuclear
in a pub between the Ithon and the Wye,
the woman with the eyes of liquid sky is
Julie Christie. Locals neither point nor stare.

No-one knows they're here. Twiggy, jamming good
in Busnant Farm. And Salman Rushdie, hiding
in a cottage on the Eppynt. Invisible beside his
dazzling minder, Good Time George.

This is where the hiders find each other.
Then themselves. And when the game is up,
the wise ones know it's time to make a move.
London. Maybe California. Cardiff will do.

*Paul Deaton*

# RED BRICK FARM

The field is furrowed,
orderly manicured like Zen-gravel.
No rain. And the swathed soil
has set to a cookie crust.

The red brick farm sits centrally,
a hub for the field's wheel
the noosing river, a May moon
pale and undistinguished,

behind, a long treeless ridge,
but for two battalions of squared-off fir,
ducking a steel girder of cloud.
The sun strikes and charges,

but the well grouped firs are firm.
They keep secrets and a night's dark
within their great thick coats.
They have long hidden pockets.

The river Wye out-pours;
far back on Plynlimon mountain a water jug has toppled:
here, nearing the end of their descent,
the waters stretch and glide.

The fidgeting trout leap acrobatically.
Under an alder on fist-sized stones
a heron holds the hour,
his dagger stabs the water with just one cut.

## Ric Hool

# THIGH-DEEP IN SNOW & THINKING: LEE HARWOOD

*During a walk in The Black Mountains, early January 2010*

The drift is 8 feet high and curled
like a surfer's dream wave
I think
they call the shape a *tube*
and
crawling thro carefully
the whole frozen moment stays intact
perfect
sudden as his verse
unfinished as his lines are completely

Two hours
Two miles
there is no hurry
no misplaced foot
A meditation begins as
breath
      step
          balance
are things considered and secret

Tracks of wildlife
A dragged-belly kill snakes downhill
swallowed
underground

But how is Brighton?
Wish you were
here       I might just
thud a snowball off your shoulder
just to see you turn
and laugh

*Paul Groves*

# AT PARTRISHOW IN THE BLACK MOUNTAINS

The sun rises over England, and sets over Wales.
We look eastwards for each new dawn, westwards
for every sunset. There is fresh blood at dusk.
It is a wonder the hills don't redden with it, the streams
run like urgent haemorrhages, clotting behind boulders,
coagulating among rock pools. The air also is unstable,
thick with invading words. Century by century
the English tongue has licked or lashed
the Welsh identity. Spin the dial of your radio:
London is here, dominant in this quiet valley
where the saint was murdered. His church
is wedded to the hillside with a ring of silence.
Its stones are those laid with effort and precision
a thousand years ago. The builders, among these trees,
these hollows, had the faces and hands of men, but the vision
of angels. Turn the radio off. Quietude returns.
Or let it play, night and day, raucous and foreign;
within a week it will have succumbed, its batteries drained.
But the stream will still be here, as will the church.
The faith will remain. The hope might even strengthen.

## Ruth Bidgood

# EDWARD BACHE ADVISES HIS SISTER

*A found poem from a letter of 1802, written from Ludlow.*

Dear Sister,
Although I have no reason
to suspect you of misconduct,
yet my affection and solicitude
will, I hope, excuse these lines
of brotherly advice.
Being visited by men
who profess themselves your admirers,
and not under protection from your parents,
you are now at the most critical period
in the life of a woman.

Young, inexperienced, unsuspicious,
fond of flattery (as what woman is not),
she too often falls a victim to those worst of men
who, with the aid of oaths, protestations,
and promise of marriage,
seduce her from the paths of virtue,
rob her of her virginity,
and leave her to lament her credulity
in the most abject state of wretchedness,
deserted by her acquaintance,
reviled and scoffed at by her enemies,
a reproach to her friends,
a disgrace to her family,
and, far worse than all of these,
condemned by her own conscience!
The remainder of her life
must be miserable indeed.

If ever you find yourself in danger
of falling into this pit,
think only of the picture I have drawn
and you will shrink with horror
from the dreadful prospect,
and reflect with pleasing terror
on your happy deliverance
from the jaws of a monster so hideous.
Again, dear sister, let me advise you
not to throw yourself away.
You are yet very young,
neither ugly nor deformed,
of a creditable family,
and not entirely destitute of fortune.
Not that I would have you consider yourself
of more consequence than you are,
but I would deter you from doing
that which is beneath you.
Your very affectionate Brother,
Edward Bache.

## Maggie Harris

# SLAVE BANGLE, WALES

In tough times, only two things rise –
hope, and the price of gold;
ushered like hymns from the tavern
full-blown with the potential of proverbs
enter the cavern of the pawnshop,
third-world lives on first-world footsteps –
leather, crepe-soles, brogues –
bringing their barter to the goblin men
before bailiffs come to the door.

The boy with the restless eyes
hip-hop on his mobile phone
his grand-dad's medals warm
on his hipbone,

the widow in the sheepskin coat
squaring her shoulders to the task
of freeing her husband's watch
from its Victorian clasp;

and the brown-skinned woman
accent weaving assonance
*pawn* to *porn*
unfolding tissue
lifted from a handbag littered
with council tax and telephone
and central heating bills.

She's been in a cavern before, in 1954
a metal-tasting darkness
with flames on a far-back wall
where her child eyes took to the light
and a Rumpelstiltskin spun St Christophers
from molten gold.

He'd hammered a pattern of sugarcane leaves
onto a ribbon of gold
curled it and wrapped it
around her mother's bones.

Now a Caribbean songbird breaks its beak against her throat
as another goblin weighs
in his cracked and calloused palm
her slave bangle
£9 for a gram –
the price of a bag of coal.

## John Barnie

# WHERE I'M FROM

Give me a tuft of sheep's wool from the Black Mountains
and a piece of dead gorse if you have any
grey and worn smooth to the touch from weather

almost woven as if someone had done it and thrown it away
and said she'd do another one another day
and the day never came and the gorse went on flowering
oil of almond infusing the air, light a sharp brittle yellow
as she passed; yes, give me the wool and the gorse if you can

the wool to be pressed to the nose for the mutton smell
the gorse to be held in the hand and turned by the fingers
a braille message but written in another tongue.

## Barney Norris

# CRICKADARN

The flock churn the grass
and the footrot claims them,
bloat of the bellies
where the bodies float in the twine-blue
depth of the pond in the wood

where the farmers throw them.
Storm across the valley,
buzzards circling,
burning of birch logs
and the earth's yearning.

## Simon Mundy

# WINTER TREACHERY AT GWAITHLA

On the bare trees the apples still hang
Shrivelled by this deep and early frost.
Pipes will puncture in their usual place,
Copper sliced by a scalpel of ice,
Winter's surgeon unwilling to wait
For the anaesthetic of lagging and heaters
To take the edge off this hidden pain.
On the back step the youngest cat
Gazes balefully at the locked door,
Willing it to open, allow the dart upstairs
To last week's warm bed, second-hand
Hot water bottle and the certainty of human care.
Only I know how callously such simple
Trust is broken.

*John Powell Ward*

# THE WYE BELOW BREDWARDINE

The banks are steep. Drought. Water too low.
Too many trees by it too, it feels. Yet
They impress heavily, this hot calm day.
Trees hang and bulge over, and peer right down.
Thirsty alders lean over, the bane of water.

Huge plate-glass windows sliding along
Horizontally, slowly rotate as they go. No
Hurry in such drift. And when flies and seeds
Hit it, dartboards widen and meet the dead
Hauteur of the banks, their raw nettle clumps.

Lower down these panes bump submerged reefs,
Lazily give, yet resist quite breaking.
Little folds and pleats adjust the Wye's surface.
Leaning over you see its tiny corkscrewings,
Like pocks on estuary mud, but down water.

Suddenly near one bank in a patch of weedy
Sunlight, a blue shoal of chub. And,
Several feet down by the bridge's piles, one
Salmon flickered deep like a neon light.
Swinging on a branch, a tyre half-submerged.

What ease has this tonnage of sedately moving
Water. Sleepily it stirs, then enfolded
With so slight a turn rolls over in bed and
Weighs sideways down again. A hundred metres
Wide. Leaves, bubbles, downy stuff, flies.

It is evening sunlight. Already. Lambs baa.
I love you, sylvan Wye, or would do so
If that were tenable, correct, and still allowed.
Instead, I say too many trees. Traherne himself
Imagined this heaven. Is there hope? Swans arrive.

## Tracey Rhys

# EN ROUTE TO HAY

We left too late, as usual in those days of sitters,
steamed the children from our corners like stamps,
headed for the mountains, hawks circling,
sheep knotted in dips.

Just after Brecon, bikes, skittering the white lines,
lean as the boy who took me skating at seventeen,
who let go my fingers hoping that I'd glide away,
a child without stabilisers.

We parted like Torville and Dean, my arms reaching
for his belt buckle until somehow, I picked up speed,
took out teens with open palms, clipped a lady, spun
an OAP, crashed into the barrier like a cub.

We laughed limp shouldered, weak as the light.
Here in the car with the windows down, there comes
the scrape of brakes; a contained sound, as if someone
trapped the rink in a bottle, screwed the cap.

Somewhere nearby, there are men on bikes
stealing their nerves for the black ice
or ploughing across without reserve,
it being too late to stop and the prize still moving.

# Ben Ray

## TALYBONT TO LLANGATTOCK

And suddenly it is summer and the world is slower,
a year lost like a coin dropped into the silty depths
as time seems to amble along the water's edge.
When sunlight lies down on the rippled surface
the roach and trout flick and shimmer
under the spotlight – sliding down to the cooler bottom
on the dim, dusky floor of the canal.
The best place to catch them is Brynich Lock, they say.
On hot days, whilst hikers sweat, defeated, on benches
the midges make the canal their private kingdom –
darting up and down with the urgency
that comes to those with only a summer left to live.
Each August there's a music festival in Crickhowell
and the distant guitar riffs nudge birds from the trees,
attempting to penetrate the recesses of brick banks –
the midges don't mind it much. They're too busy
carving the air up in infinite mosaics.

## Gareth Writer-Davies
# MUSHROOMS

*Gallt yr Ancr, Meifod*

last night, I heard the cows mooing
like a man trying to start a chainsaw

my host said, they had probably eaten magic
and tomorrow's milk would have a real kick to it

the hill of the anchorite
is fiery with autumn bracken, as I take the steep way

of hawthorn and rabbits
my eyes large with last night's candlenight

the soft eruptions of agaric on toast
that had I known

I would have set aside
my portion for the cat, which tracks me now like a panther

is this how the cloistered life began
waiting for the master?

last night, I heard the owl snore
and buried myself in blankets

my eyes are large
the path between the trees narrows.

## Catherine Fisher

# SEVERN BORE

Somewhere out there the sea has shrugged its shoulders.
Grey-green masses slip, rise, gather
to a ripple and a wave, purposeful, arrowing up
arteries of the land. Brown and sinuous, supple
as an otter, nosing upstream under the arching
bridge, past Chepstow, Lydney, Berkeley where a king
screamed; Westbury, where old men
click stopwatches with grins of satisfaction;
slopping into the wellingtons of watchers,
swamping the nests of coots, splashing binoculars.
And so to Minsterworth meadows where Ivor Gurney's ghost
walks in sunlight, unforgotten; past lost
lanes, cow-trodden banks, nudging the reeds,
lifting the lank waterweed,
flooding pills, backwaters, bobbing the floats
of fishermen, the undersides of leaves and boats,
and gliding, gliding over Cotswold's flawed
reflection, the sun swelling, the blue sky scored
with ripples, fish and dragonfly, stirred
by the drip and cloop of oars; and finally, unheard,
washing into backstreets of the town to lie
at the foot of the high
cathedral, prostrate, breathless,
pilgrim from a far place,
refugee
from the ominous petulance of the sea.

## Philip Gross

# SEVERN SONG

*for John Karl Gross 1919-2011*

The Severn was brown and the Severn was blue —
not this-then-that, not either-or,
no mixture. Two things can be true.
The hills were clouds and the mist was a shore.

The Severn was water, the water was mud
whose eddies stood and did not fill,
The kind of water that's thicker than blood.
The river was flowing, the flowing was still,

the tide-rip the sound of dry fluttering wings
with waves that did not break or fall.
We were two of the world's small particular things.
We were old, we were young, we were no age at all,

For a moment not doing, nor coming undone —
words gained, words lost, till who's to say
which was the father, which was the son,
a week, or fifty years, away.

But the water said *earth* and the water said sky.
We were everyone we'd ever been or would be,
every angle of light that says *You*, that says *I*,
and the sea was the river, the river the sea.

*Claire Williamson*

# LLANCAUT/LLAN CEWYDD

Upstream from the castle's sheer defence,
the Wye's spoon-tip nose is nudged to a tidal simmer.

A pine cone's throw from the border, I live with one eye
on the truculent Severn, another on the equivocal Afon Gwy.

Sleeping on this green strip between these rivers,
I dream hybrid dreams, tilting to England, to Wales.

Roofless St James', on the banks of Lancaut,
once stood on Welsh land, now by English saltmarsh

below the sheltering wood, Ban-y-Gor, *over the corners*,
where a water-bound community found the hush

of limestone cliffs, lapidary snails, otters, seals,
soothing horse-heal, hellebore and the rare checker tree.

This deep-pocketed place feeds me
with the sound of shifting salmon, the stir of reeds.

*Paul Henry*

# BOY RUNNING

The canal tilts him back and fore
like a boat in a toy pen
or the bubble in a spirit-level
that never quite finds its middle.

There are worse ways to grow tall
under the rustling sun and rain
between bridges 14 and 21

to outlive an owl, a drake, a hawk
where no two leaves blow the same way
and pumpkin lanterns moor for the night.

Run, boy running, run
past the sighing old man
and his blind Labrador,
the foal in her wire necklace.

Run, between east and west,
spring and autumn, dawn and dusk.
Is it your breath now or mine
deep inside your chest?

There are worse ways to never settle
in full flight, to be loved.
Run, my shadow, run.
Run but always stay in sight.

An owl cries, deep inside the trees.
The canal's glass is full of moonlight.

# Nicholas Murray

# YGGDRASIL

*In Norse mythology the ancient evergreen tree of fate,*
*under which the gods sit in council*
*and which upholds the universe; a yew, or an ash.*
    A Dictionary of English Plant Names, Geoffrey Grigson

Well, which is it? Yew or ash?
Strong enough to bear the full weight
of this struggling universe
that we are helping to destruction.

Grey day in Radnor,
the shaken sheet of rain,
flicked forward by the great ash
that towers above my house

where the nuthatch zigzags
and small twigs, knuckled,
fall to the grass, dry out
and are broken with a snap.

I cannot hear the gods,
murmuring in conference.
They are not quarrelsome Greeks
but Northerners, taciturn,

leaning on the pommels
of their long swords,
moved to speech
slowly, with reluctance,

baffled by the madness
of the occupants
of this world of men
and women

under the dripping ash
with its bark of silver grey
and those tipped buds of black
where the leaf will open.

## Richard Gwyn

# BORDER COUNTRY

I sit in the woods above my sister's house. The border passes through her land, an invisible boundary. How to define its nature? A border is an idea wedded to a geography. It implies a shift of consciousness, a change of order. That is why the light is as it is; shadowy, circumspect, dappled now that there is weather. It skirts a quiet and ceremonious landscape in which to bury things; unclaimed artefacts, memory, the particles left behind on waking. Dream sediment. This is a zone of curtains and unseen partitions. A landscape which provides the thread between the deep uncertainty of sleep and the fragile certainty of waking. Wandering along this borderline, following the trail between one country and another, is all I've ever done.

## Emma van Woerkom

# WATER BREAK-ITS-NECK

We speak your name like myth
wrung out through roots of bracken
a terror spawned of mountain rain
running crazed seams down the dark nape of rock
racing to sharpen your rabid tongue and
over-spilling blanched lips as mad laughter.

In the down-draft we feel Welsh-wind draw breath
like a throat caught, just as the razor bites;
released through the gorge your haemorrhage of water
in threshing skinned air we shiver to the thrum
of mass-speed-of-light-squared crashing each horizontal
and clattering like shaking bones in a cup.

Cleaved creature, all explosions and white-water tantrums;
sky-cauldron cascading with restless momentum.
But we stop, look back, carve names onto shale.
Push old copper coins into sodden black bark.
Pray in secret to gods for another man's luck,
while the Future slips into the belly of a brook.

N.B. Water-Break-its-Neck is a spectacular waterfall located within
the Radnor Forest. At its base people continue in the ancient tradition
of writing name on stones and pushing coin offerings into the bark of
wishing trees.

*Fiona Sampson*

# MONTGOMERY ORCHARD

Who is this
who comes barefoot
over the shining
grass over
clover and grass
each shining stem
and leaf white
with frost is it
morning it is
the first morning
who comes walking
barefoot on the grass
that bends and bends
under his feet
this is the rhythm
of prayer this
is how we always
knew it would be
bare feet in the bare
orchard
feet in the ginnels
of the grass
is this how
it will be walking
through the frost
under bare trees
when we are alone?

*Charles Wilkinson*

# ENGLYNION WITH GNOMES AND BUTTERFLIES

*The wise men all fear the withdrawn request.*
  Wing-surf caught in the slant
  of light breaking through trees.
Where white butterflies foolflight –

*Know that your details are kept in the cloud.*
  The speckled wood is brown
  & has yellow dots of code.
When looking through its eyespots –

*A foe watches though you close the window.*
  Orange tips glow with pointed
  flames' flutterturn through spring.
Behind the snow & ash screen –

*The darkest ravens always work off-line.*
  A duel of butterflies
  seen as it crosses the moon.
Though night wipes the stars gleaming –

*An old spider lost the key in the web.*
  Some threads of sunlight stitched
  into wings kept under glass.
Whilst too delicate to fly –

*The padlock is for the insecure dream.*
  Known results of desire
  traced to the forest floor.
As loving shadows on silk –

*Jonathan Edwards*

# ANATOMY

These shoulder blades are Snowdon, the Brecon Beacons.
Walk gently on them. This spine is the A470;
these palms are Ebbw, Wye, Sirhowy. This tongue

is Henry VIII's Act of Union, these lungs
pneumoconiosis, these rumbling guts
the Gurnos, this neck Dic Penderyn. This manner

of speaking is my children, my children's children.
These vital organs are Nye Bevan, this liver
Richard Burton, this blood my father. These eyes

have been underground for generations; now
they're adjusting to the light. This gap-toothed smile
is the Severn Bridge, seen from the English side.